No. 6626. Prescription Scales. A polished cherry or walnut box, with drawer: has pillar and 6-in. beam, 2 ½-inch pans and full set of weights; weight, 1½ lbs. Price......$2.25

No. 6626

No. 6627. Prescription Scales with pillar and 8 inch beam, on polished walnut box with drawer, nickel plated, pans 2¾ in diameter, brass work lacquered; has full set of weights. Price............$3.75
Scale No. 6627 can be taken apart and packed in drawer of the stand.

FLASH LAMP.

No. 6630. The "James" Flash Lamp is the simplest yet most practical device ever invented for burning flash light powders of all kinds. It dispenses entirely with the use of alcohols gasoline, etc. The powder is ignited with a common parlor match by simply pulling the trigger with the finger when you are ready. The action lights the match which is forced by a spring into the powder in the flash pan exploding it. The charge of powder can be governed to suit the requirements. Price.....................$1.60

Harvard Book Holders.

An ornament to the home, office and library. No wood-work used in their construction. A holder we highly recommend. The sides are operated by double acting springs, the book being firmly clamped while closed, and resting upon a level surface when open. The adjustment to books of differ-sizes and the inclination to any angle or slant are effected by a single screw. They are adjustable to different heights, and are easily set up. They are warranted not to break or get out of order with ordinary use, and after years of proper use will be as good as new.
52000 Complete with casters and revolving book shelf, Nickel Plated and highly polished or antique copper. Price............$3.85
52002 Complete with casters and Revolving Book Shelf and finished in rubber, Japan or bronze. Price.................................$2.10
52003 One same style as No. 52000 but no shelf or casters. Price...................$1.85

Dictionary and Book Holders.

Cannot be broken with ordinary us-age. The edges of the covers are protected by felt-lined guards, and the rests are so made that the book cannot

to break or get out of order with ordinary use, and after years of proper use will be as good as new.
52000 Complete with casters and revolving book shelf, Nickel Plated and highly polished or antique copper. Price............$3.85
52002 Complete with casters and Revolving Book Shelf and finished in rubber, Japan or bronze. Price.................................$2.10
52003 One same style as No. 52000 but no shelf or casters. Price......................$1.85

Noyes' Dictionary and Book Holders.

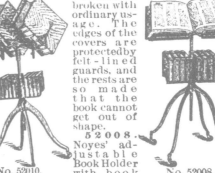

Cannot be broken with ordinary us-age. The edges of the covers are protected by felt-lined guards, and the rests are so made that the book cannot get out of shape.
52008. Noyes' adjustable Book Holder with book rack, bronze. Price..............................$2.10

No. 52010.   No. 52008.

52010 With Book Rack to hold two volumes, bronze. Price..$3.25

Globes.

For offices, homes, libraries, or the school room these globes **are the best in the country** at the price we offer them.
It would be impossible to place too much emphasis upon the fact that the covers used upon these globes, all sizes, **are from new plates.** Every improvement in engraving, printing, coloring and mounting the maps has received **critical attention,** and the latest geographical changes are correctly shown.
A copy of the **Globe Manual** will accompany each globe.
The Manual Gives Explanations of the Terms Used in Geography and Astronomy, and the phenomena of mathematical geography, including **temperature and ocean currents,** and forty-six problems on the use of globes, with rules and illustrative examples; also several valuable tables.

52012. Full Mounted.   **52014. Meridian.**

Government and Politics

LIFE IN AMERICA 100 YEARS AGO

Government and Politics

John C. Havens

Chelsea House Publishers
Philadelphia

CHELSEA HOUSE PUBLISHERS
Editorial Director: Richard Rennert
Production Manager: Pamela Loos
Art Director: Sara Davis
Picture Editor: Judy Hasday

This book is dedicated to my grandfather, A. Warren Dayton, whose infectious passion for knowledge has been an inspiration to his students and family for more than half a century.

LIFE IN AMERICA 100 YEARS AGO
Senior Editor: John Ziff

Staff for *GOVERNMENT AND POLITICS*
Associate Editor: Therese De Angelis
Editorial Assistant: Kristine Brennan
Designer: Terry Mallon
Picture Researcher: Sandy Jones

3 5 7 9 8 6 4 2
Library of Congress Cataloging-in-Publication Data

Havens, John C.
    Government and politics/John C. Havens.
    96 pp. cm.—(Life in America 100 years ago)
    Includes bibliographical references and index.
    Summary: An overview of government policies, presidential elections, and the changing political climate from the aftermath of the Civil War to the beginning of the twentieth century.
    ISBN 0-7910-2847-X (hardcover)
    1. United States—Politics and government—1865-1900—Juvenile literature.
    [1. United States—Politics and government—1865-1900.] I. Title. II. Series.
E661.H38 1996   96-35234
973—dc20
                                                                                          CIP
                                                                                           AC

CONTENTS

LIFE IN AMERICA 100 YEARS AGO

Communication

Education

Frontier Life

Government and Politics

Health and Medicine

Industry and Business

Law and Order

Manners and Customs

Sports and Recreation

Transportation

Urban Life

Government and Politics

The Gilded Age

THE CIVIL WAR OF 1861-65 DEVASTATED THE UNITED STATES. In the aftermath of the country's bloodiest war, Americans faced the enormous task of reuniting the shattered country economically, socially, and politically. Confederate states were placed under military occupation by the victorious North. Scores of enslaved African Americans—until this time considered property by southern plantation owners and many others—were set free; thus slaveholders lost their laborers as well as their livelihoods, while newly freed blacks searched for other means of making a living.

During the era immediately following the Civil War—the Reconstruction—the nation's economy was practically rebuilt: new taxes, new currency, and new banking systems were established. The beginning of the machine age, or the Industrial Revolution, earlier in the century had already transformed the economy. Machines produced more goods more quickly than did manual laborers, and the development of new methods of transportation, such as railroad lines, brought national prosperity by the end of the 1870s.

After the Civil War, President Andrew Johnson granted widespread pardons and amnesties that aroused bitterness among his original supporters. The famous 19th-century political cartoonist Thomas Nast reflected this sentiment in an 1866 drawing of Johnson as Iago (from Shakespeare's play *Othello*). Nast is remembered today primarily for developing the image of the Republican party as an elephant.

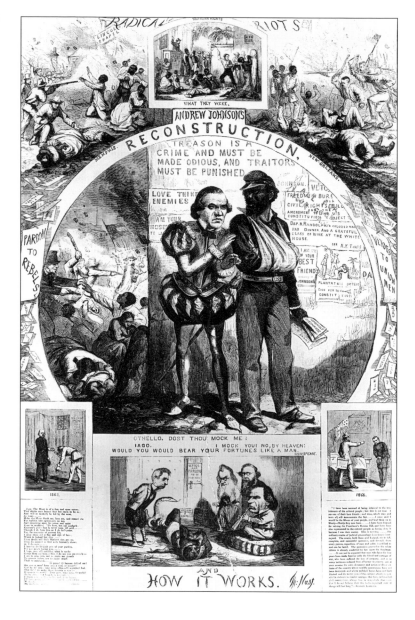

But these changes also brought many difficulties. Increased populations in industrial centers created overcrowded, unhealthy living conditions, and factory employees faced the added hazards of working with machines. Farming became less crucial to the national economy and business became more important—and more influential in politics. Corporations began to combine, forming "trusts" to reduce competition with similar businesses. By the end of the Reconstruction, political corruption and favoritism were commonplace.

Contemporary historian Henry Adams referred to the years after Reconstruction as "poor in purpose and barren in results. . . . One might search the whole list of Congress, Judiciary, and Executive during the twenty-five years 1870-1895 and find little but damaged reputations." This period is often referred to as the Gilded Age, after a book of the same title by humorist Mark Twain and Charles Dudley Warner. One of the novel's characters, Colonel Beriah Sellers, is forever involved in underhanded schemes to secure political favors. In Colonel Sellers, Twain and Warner satirized a type of American politician that became common during this era, one who was more concerned with influence and successful office seeking than with moral or ethical issues.

A prime example was Democratic organizer William Marcy "Boss" Tweed of Tammany Hall in New York City. Originally a patriotic society founded in 1789 by a former soldier of the revolutionary war, Tammany eventually became involved in politics, and beginning in the early 1800s it became deeply enmeshed in corruption and cover-ups.

By 1868, Tammany Hall had become the seat of power for the Democratic party in New York, with Boss Tweed as its new leader. By various means over the next three years, he and his associates, known as the Tweed Ring, would plunder vast sums of money from New York taxpayers. One scheme, for example, involved the construction of a new courthouse, which was begun in 1868 at a planned cost of $500,000.

One of the most notorious examples of the political corruption and government favoritism of the Gilded Age was Tammany Hall in New York City. Under William Marcy "Boss" Tweed, depicted here as an enthroned tiger, Tammany Hall became the seat of power for the Democratic party in New York. Boss Tweed robbed the city of millions of dollars before being jailed in 1873.

THE CEREMONY OF SUBMISSION.

In 1871, the building was still incomplete, and the cost had risen to $8 million. Clearly, the money had not been spent on the courthouse. After the *New York Times* exposed the Tweed Ring, Tweed was arrested and sentenced to 12 years in prison.

Around the same time that Tweed and his associates were robbing the New York treasury, the United States Congress was facing a scandal of its own. In 1864, Thomas Durant, vice president of the Union Pacific Railroad, purchased the construction company hired to build a railroad link from Omaha to Promontory Point, Utah, for Union Pacific. Durant renamed the construction company Crédit Mobilier of America. Because the railroad company owned Crédit Mobilier itself, the government's extensive financial support only increased Union Pacific's profits.

Ulysses S. Grant, one of the best-known generals of the Civil War, was elected president in 1868 and served for eight years. Though he was never implicated himself, Grant's presidency was marked by graft, scandal, and corruption involving his vice president, Schuyler Colfax, his personal secretary, Orville Babcock, and many other high-level officials.

This stereoscope photograph shows a railroad snow shed under construction on the Union Pacific Railroad line in Aspen, Colorado. During the half century between the end of the Civil War and the start of World War I—known as the Golden Age of American railroading—over 219,000 miles of new track was laid, most of it across the frontier line of the West.

In 1867, Oakes Ames, a Massachusetts congressman and stockholder of Crédit Mobilier, attempted to influence legislation that was favorable to Union Pacific. In an effort to avoid an investigation into Union Pacific and Crédit Mobilier, Ames distributed shares in the companies to government office holders at vastly reduced prices, allowing them to make huge profits.

During the months leading up to the presidential election of 1872, the scandal became public. No fewer than 15 leading politicians, including Vice President Schuyler Colfax, Representative (later President) James A. Garfield, and House Speaker James G. Blaine were implicated (suspected of being involved).

Other scandals involved President Grant's secretary of war, W. W. Belknap, who had accepted bribes from Indian traders at army posts in the West, and General Robert Schenck, minister to London, who had sold stock in worthless mines to unsuspecting Englishmen. The term "political machine"—an appropriate image for the industrial age —was coined during this period to describe the startlingly organized manner in which political groups engaged in corruption. One of Tweed's assistants, Peter Sweeney, attributed the success of the Tweed Ring to "the completeness of its organization and the thoroughness of its discipline. . . . The organization works with the precision of a well-regulated machine."

Despite—or perhaps because of—the political confusion and corruption of this era, Americans went to the polls in record numbers: roughly 70 to 80 percent of those qualified to vote participated in presidential elections during the Gilded Age. Believing that personal political involvement was important in settling national issues, many citizens regularly attended rallies and party speeches, immersing themselves in the workings of government.

Partly because of the public's fondness for such gatherings, the American politician underwent a transformation during the Gilded Age. In an election, the speaking skills, physical appearance, style of dress, and personality of a candidate became important; a favorable presentation would often secure more votes than would an impressive record.

In the presidential election of 1884, for example, Senator James G. Blaine of Maine presented himself as a true gentleman and a fine speaker. Despite his suspected involvement in the Crédit Mobilier scandal, Blaine was nominated by Robert G. Ingersoll in 1876 with the famous "plumed knight" speech:

On May 10, 1869, the first transcontinental railroad was completed with a "Golden Spike" ceremony, shown here, at Promontory Point in Utah Territory.

Like an armed warrior, like a plumed knight, James G. Blaine marched down the halls of American Congress and threw his shining lance full and fair against the brazen forehead of the defamers of his country and maligners of honor.

Because it became important to make a strong impression on voters, grand and passionate words like Ingersoll's were common in turn-of-the-century political speech making. Senator Roscoe Conkling of New York, the leader of the Stalwart party, a group of Republicans who remained hostile to Southern interests after the Civil War, described politics as a kind of church to which one must dedicate oneself entirely. "If any church is worth belonging to," Conkling stated, "it is worth belonging to not a little. That is true in politics as in religion."

The Republican party held power in the Northeast and Midwest, as well as in New England. Aligned with the more evangelical Protestant churches, it considered itself the party of progress, concerned with temperance, moral reform, and education. Republicans decried the Democrats' habit of "waving the bloody shirt," of constantly emphasizing the divisiveness of the Civil War and the harsh policies of Reconstruction. As eloquent in his support of the Republican party as he was of Blaine, Ingersoll stated that the party "has in it the elements of growth. It is full of hope. It anticipates. The Democratic party remembers."

Since Abraham Lincoln, who had been president during the Civil War, was a Republican, the party also claimed that, as the "abolition party," it had saved the Union. Republicans would continue to win most of the presidential elections of the Gilded Age: Ulysses S. Grant, Rutherford B. Hayes, James Garfield, and Benjamin Harrison.

The Republican hold on the presidency, however, remained firm more for economic than for ideological reasons. In farm states such as Indiana, Illinois, and Ohio, where agricultural interests were strong, Republicans won favor by advocating high protective tariffs on imported corn; corn was a staple of U.S. farmers.

The Republican party was hardly cohesive, however. Factions such as Liberals, Radicals, Half-Breeds (or dissenters), and Stalwarts threatened to tear apart the "party of liberty." Donn Piatt, a contemporary political commentator, noted these fractures in an article in the *Cincinnati Commercial Gazette* on June 9, 1870:

> I am forced to say that there is no more cohesion, beyond mere office holding and public plunder, in the Republican party than there is in a rope of sand. . . . The Republican party in Congress is composed of factions in such deadly antagonisms to each other that the hate among them is more intense than that given the Democrats.

In contrast to the Republicans, Democrats of the Reconstruction period favored states' rights and limited government, and were popular with Midwest and Southwest voters, as well as with Southern whites; the South's longing for separation had not died with the end of the Civil War.

Democrats favored governmental reform. Catholics and fundamentalist Protestants were drawn to this party of "old simplicity and purity and frugality." They believed that local government should have more control than the federal government, and for the most part adhered to Andrew Jackson's antimonopoly platform. As Senator James Beck of Kentucky stated:

There is that contemptible word Nation—a word which no good
Democrat uses when he can find any other, and when forced to use it
utters it in disgust. This is not a Nation: we are free and independent States.

But for all the maneuvering and corruption, the Republican and
Democratic parties remained relatively equal in power during the
Gilded Age. Although Republicans held on to the presidency from 1869
to 1885, the Democrats generally controlled the Senate during this period.
Moreover, between 1872 and 1896, no president won office with a
majority of the popular vote.

Because each party catered to specific regions and interest groups
in the United States, presidential and vice-presidential candidates
were customarily chosen not only for their political records but also
for successfully appealing to the widest possible spectrum of interest
groups. In some ways, this prevented one group from unreasonable
influence on the candidates.

In fact, the founders of the Constitution had in mind this careful
balance of interests. In a series of essays known as the *Federalist Papers*
(1787-88), James Madison, a member of the Constitutional Convention
and later U.S. president, maintained that a balanced federal government
required a fair representation of varied political interests. During the
Gilded Age, Americans took this to heart and began demanding that
potential candidates for office publicly disclose their views.

As a result of this trend, and because the Democratic and Republican
parties held comparatively equal power, successful candidates were
those whose views most closely matched their party's platform. In this
way, the two-party, or bipartisan, system that we know today was
established. American historian Henry Adams would remark on this

Though charming and personable with a gift for speech making, James G. Blaine, the "plumed knight," was suspected of involvement in the Crédit Mobilier scandal and made an enemy of Roscoe Conkling, leader of the powerful "Stalwart" faction of the Republican party. He was denied the party's nomination in the 1876 and 1880 presidential elections but became secretary of state under James A. Garfield in 1881.

phenomenon: "[N]o real principle divides us, some queer mechanical balance holds the two parties even. . . . in democratic politics, parties tend to an equilibrium." Though other parties have been established throughout American history, many have found it necessary to align with Republican or Democratic policies to build any real political strength—and none have lasted as long as these two parties.

The two branches of Congress reflected the apparent stalemate between the major parties. The House of Representatives and the Senate seemed at times to revert to chaos and disorder. In the House, members would carry on conversations or even walk about the chamber in utter disregard of colleagues addressing the assembly. At times, members were forced to leave their seats and surround the representative who was speaking, because the clamor made it impossible to hear otherwise. The Senate, although more restrained than the unruly House, had difficulty achieving consensus on policy matters, because individual senators tended to show more political independence than House members. Although tenuous alliances were sometimes forged over specific issues, they often dissolved as the issues were settled. So fractious was the Senate that Woodrow Wilson called it "merely a body of individual critics."

Northern Republicans and southern Democrats alike were affected by the devastation of the Civil War. The sweeping changes of a ravaged —but recovering—United States threatened to overwhelm the country's political system.

Mudslingers and Mugwumps

SECURING POLITICAL POWER AND SATISFYING IMPORTANT constituents became the driving forces of both parties in the years following the Civil War. In the struggle to dominate national politics, significant policy changes were rare. Political candidates attacked opponents with such intensity that the term "mudslinging" was coined to describe the kind of slanderous accusations regularly hurled at candidates by members of the opposing party.

The public expressed its frustration over this situation in some-times comical ways. On November 7, 1874, for example, the popular periodical *Harper's Weekly* published an illustration by a well-known cartoonist, Thomas Nast. The sketch shows a forest filled with animals —representing various newspapers, states, and political issues— scattering in fear from a braying donkey clothed in a lion's skin labeled "Caesarism" (dictatorship). Among the frightened animals is an elephant, labeled "The Republican Vote," about to fall into a pit of "Southern Claims Chaos" covered by loose and splintering planks.

Like the donkey, which first represented Democrat Andrew Jackson and later the Democratic party itself, the elephant characterization stuck —and political cartoonists and commentators still use these caricatures to represent the two major parties.

The process of electing a president and vice president takes place on two levels. One, of course, is the system whereby each American citizen votes for his or her favorite candidate. But what many do not know is that they are actually voting for "electors," who have already pledged to vote for that candidate.

Before a presidential election, each political party within each state selects special voters, or electors, equal in number to the state's congressional delegation—representatives and senators. Every state then casts one electoral vote—a combination of all the votes of the electors— on an all-or-none basis. That is, the candidate—and party—who wins the majority of electoral votes in that state wins the combined vote. (Though electors normally promise to vote for their party's nominee, they are not required to do so.) During the popular election, then, voters choose these electors, and the candidates receiving the majority of the total electoral vote in the United States are elected.

No system is perfect, however. Because all of a state's electoral votes go to the winner, it is possible that presidential and vice-presidential candidates can be elected even with fewer popular votes than their opponents. And that is just what happened in the 1876 presidential election.

That year, Rutherford B. Hayes of Ohio was nominated as the Republican candidate. A three-term governor of Ohio, Hayes had instituted reforms in prisons and mental hospitals, in poor-relief bureaus, and in the Ohio school system. While he was governor, he was instrumental in Ohio's ratification of the Fifteenth Amendment, which protected the right of African Americans to vote.

Samuel J. Tilden, the Democratic nominee, was also known as a reformer. As chairman of the New York State Democratic Committee and later governor of New York, he headed the campaign to overthrow the infamous Tweed Ring that controlled New York City politics.

Early in the vote counting, Tilden appeared to have won, with 184 electoral votes—only one short of a majority. Hayes had 165 electoral votes. In the Republican-controlled states of Florida, Louisiana, and South Carolina, however, 19 electoral votes (plus one from Oregon) appeared questionable. Meanwhile, Tilden received 4,287,670 popular votes to Hayes's 4,035,924.

Republicans, however, would not concede the election. Because they controlled the federal troops occupying the South during the Reconstruction, Republicans were able to hold on to southern states for Hayes by illegally overseeing "returning" boards, who reviewed election returns for fairness. In this way, they managed to eliminate enough Tilden votes to give all the disputed states to Hayes.

Republicans were not the only politicians involved in corruption. Anti-abolitionist southern Democrats conducted their own campaign of intimidation, threatening southern blacks (who, only six years earlier, had received legal protection to vote by the Fifteenth Amendment) and driving them from the polls in an effort to increase the percentage of pro-southern Democrat votes.

The 15-member special Electoral Commission, comprising five representatives each from the House, the Senate, and the Supreme Court (eight Republicans and seven Democrats), was formed to decide on the disputed returns. On February 1, 1877—three months after the election—both houses of Congress began counting electoral votes in alphabetical order by state, referring Florida's vote to the commission. Nearly a month later, the commission, by a vote of 8 to 7, awarded the electors of Florida and all other disputed states to Hayes. Thus Tilden, despite receiving more popular votes than Hayes, lost the election.

25

A political cartoon from Birmingham, Alabama, which not only depicts the fierce hostility of defeated southern slaveholders after the Civil War, but also suggests dire consequences for freed blacks should federal troops be recalled from the South.

Republican Rutherford B. Hayes was elected in one of the most corrupt presidential elections in American history. He eventually struck a compromise with southern Democrats, agreeing to end federal occupation of the South in exchange for their political support.

In a conciliatory move that became known as the Compromise of 1877, southern Democratic congressmen agreed to back Hayes if he promised to end federal occupation of the South, especially of Louisiana and South Carolina. The congressmen were anxious to renew ties with northern businessmen, believing it would pave the way for their return to power. Over the next eight years, Tilden and his New York and southern associates would retain control of the national Democratic party, and in 1884 would be instrumental in achieving the first Democratic presidential victory in more than two decades.

Roscoe Conkling, leader of the Stalwart Republicans. As undisputed head of the New York state political machine, Conkling engaged in bitter power struggles with party members who advocated civil-service reform. As president, Rutherford B. Hayes refused to recognize Conkling's claims to the control of New York federal appointments. Conkling resigned his Senate seat in 1881 in protest of President James A. Garfield's continuing reforms.

Democratic presidential candidate Winfield Scott Hancock as the biblical Samson against the "Republican Philistines." A Union general and Civil War hero, Hancock was ridiculed by Republicans for being politically naive. In the closest presidential election of the century, Hancock lost to James A. Garfield, who was favored by less than 10,000 popular votes but received the majority of electoral votes.

But President Hayes ultimately paid a high price for the compromise. The way in which he was elected drew steady criticism throughout his term from opponents who taunted him as "Old 8 to 7" (referring to the Electoral Commission's deciding votes). A distinguished Civil War veteran elected to Congress while still in service, Hayes nonetheless labored as president to restore integrity and fairness to the office and to the federal government.

One of Hayes's most important achievements as president was his reform of the country's civil-service system. Up to this time, civil servants —civilian government employees appointed, not elected, to office— were selected by the president based on their individual qualifications. By the early 19th century, it had become customary to choose appointees based on party affiliation, regardless of skills. This "spoils system" (so named from the refrain "To the victor belong the spoils") reached an extreme during the Reconstruction era.

In June 1877, Hayes issued an executive order prohibiting civil servants from active involvement in politics. He removed those who had been appointed for political gain and outlawed political contributions as a means of securing positions.

Not surprisingly, the new policy met with fierce opposition from those who favored the spoils system. Its most vocal opponent was Stalwart Republican senator Roscoe Conkling of New York, the undisputed head of the state's political machine, who controlled all of its federal appointments.

The Republican party's divisiveness persisted into 1880, when conflicts arose over the party's choice of presidential candidate. Stalwarts, led by Roscoe Conkling, supported Ulysses S. Grant for a third term. But a rival faction nominated John Sherman instead. Ballot after ballot failed to produce a majority vote. Finally, Sherman's supporters nominated James A. Garfield, Sherman's campaign manager, after 36 ballots. Though Garfield opposed his own nomination, the "dark horse" candidate (one who is unexpectedly nominated) won the nomination by a 399-to-306 majority.

To conciliate the defeated Stalwarts, Republicans chose for vice president Chester A. Arthur, a customhouse appointee of Roscoe Conkling who, though personally honest, was responsible for awarding thousands of New York civil-service jobs to Republicans.

In the 1884 presidential campaign, Democratic candidate Grover Cleveland and vice-presidential candidate Thomas A. Hendricks ran on a campaign of honesty and reform. Cleveland and Hendricks are pictured below smaller portraits showing American patriots.

Meanwhile, Democrats wanted to avoid Republican accusations of keeping alive the political wounds of the Civil War. They nominated former Union commander Winfield Scott Hancock as their candidate. In the closest election of the century, Garfield won—with a popular vote of only 48.5 percent—having received 214 electoral votes to Hancock's 155.

Garfield had been in office only a few months when, on July 2, 1881, he was shot in the back while vacationing in New England. The assassin, Charles Guiteau, who declared himself a Stalwart, had unsuccessfully sought a federal appointment, and wanted to eliminate Garfield so that Arthur could assume office. On September 19, more than two months after the shooting, James Garfield died. The next day, Chester A. Arthur took the oath of office as president of the United States.

Though Conkling and other Stalwarts expected the new president to revert to the spoils system of civil-service appointments, Arthur surprised many by continuing Hayes's reforms. In January 1883, he signed into law the Pendleton Civil Service Act, the first significant step toward the "merit system" of appointing civil servants.

The Pendleton Act established the three-member Civil Service Commission to determine the specifics of a category known as "classified services," constituting about 14 percent of all government jobs. To secure a classified service position, an applicant was required to earn, or merit, the job by passing a standard competitive examination.

Arthur's reform policies alienated former Republican allies and he was never able to gain control of his party. For this reason, he was not renominated for office in 1884. Instead, Republicans championed James G. Blaine of Maine—the "plumed knight." Though a fine orator, Blaine's alleged involvement in railroad scandals caused Democrats to mock him as the "plumed knave."

Nor did all Republicans approve of Blaine. During the party's convention in June 1884, a group of Republican reformists who opposed Blaine's nomination eventually deserted the party to vote for Grover Cleveland (a Democrat). Charles Dana, editor of the *New York Sun*, labeled this group "mugwumps"—from the Algonquin term "mugquomp," meaning "big chief." He used the name to suggest that reformist Republicans thought themselves better than those who voted according to their party affiliation.

Cleveland had attracted the attention of his party three years earlier as mayor of Buffalo, New York, when he acted on his campaign promises of honesty and economy and proved himself a competent administrator. Though he consistently opposed the Tammany Hall political machine—antagonizing a powerful faction in his own party—he was nevertheless suggested as a nominee for governor in 1882. Cleveland's reputation for political independence eventually won him the nomination—and the election.

The presidential campaign of 1884 was a bitter mudslinging contest. Among other personal and political accusations, Democrats published correspondence between Blaine and others that allegedly proved that he was involved in illegal land-grant schemes eight years earlier. Republicans countered by revealing that Cleveland was the father of an illegitimate child, born of a Buffalo woman named Maria Halperin (the candidate had already acknowledged this fact and had accepted responsibility for the child).

Nevertheless, aided by Republican mugwump support, Grover Cleveland won the majority of both electoral and popular votes, thus securing the first Democratic victory in 24 years.

One of the first problems Cleveland faced in his presidency was that of political patronage. Like his Republican predecessor, Cleveland

This 1882 political cartoon depicts Republican James G. Blaine being "tantalized" by the promise of a presidential nomination in 1884 but held back by his tarnished political record.

strongly supported the Pendleton Act. But many Democrats who had been loyal to Cleveland during his campaign were eager to secure positions in the new administration. At the same time, the reformers among them were reluctant to replace completely the Republicans already in office.

At first, Cleveland resisted the demands of his party's favor seekers. But under pressure, he eventually gave in and swept out of office two-thirds of the federal employees under his control. To appease Democratic reformers, however, he nearly doubled the number of available classified civil-service positions.

Though he was known as a reformer, Cleveland emphasized moral integrity and corrective—not progressive—action to improve the federal government. Like many Americans during this period, Cleveland believed that each citizen was entitled to justice and honesty in government, but that did not extend to social services or federal involvement in their daily lives.

One of President Cleveland's most important calls for change addressed the tariff issue. Most Republicans favored a protective tariff—a high tax that would discourage foreign traders and thus reduce competition for Americans. But Cleveland and other Democrats believed that outside competition kept the American economy healthy, and therefore they advocated a low, or "revenue," tariff—one that would bring in funds but would not discourage foreign trade.

The president claimed that the protective tariff also raised consumer prices and contributed to the development of trusts. He believed that government aid—like government regulation—should be limited. A high tariff, he said, interfered with the "natural law" of economics and promoted an unacceptable "paternalism" (or fatherly relationship) on the part of the federal government toward its citizens.

By this time, the United States Treasury had amassed a huge surplus of funds from protective tariffs and excise taxes (internal taxes on the manufacture, sale, or consumption of domestic products). Calling the Treasury "a hoarding place for money needlessly withdrawn from trade and the people's use," Cleveland called for a greatly reduced tariff.

Cleveland drew the public's attention to this issue by doing what no president had ever done: he devoted his entire annual congressional message to the subject in 1887. But his reforms were never thoroughly adopted. In July of 1888, the Mills Bill, containing only moderate reductions in tariff rates, was passed by the House. Soon after, Republicans introduced a protectionist measure in the Senate in an effort to avoid compromise on the issue.

Perhaps Cleveland's greatest accomplishment was to restore the power of the presidency. During the Reconstruction period, Congress had attained dominance over the president, so that by the time Cleveland was elected, Republican senators held all but complete control over national politics. The Tenure of Office Act, passed by Congress over President Andrew Johnson's veto in 1867, required that the president have the Senate's consent before removing any officeholder who had been appointed with Senate approval.

Reluctant to relinquish its hold, the Senate demanded that Cleveland inform it of all dismissals and nominations for offices. He refused, claiming that the president retains a constitutional right to withhold from Congress any information of a personal or confidential nature. When Republican senators threatened to block all appointments, Cleveland once again made an unprecedented move: he appealed directly to the American people. Finally, in March of 1887, Congress repealed the Tenure of Office Act.

By forcefully maintaining his views, Cleveland earned a reputation for leadership and independence, and his gruff integrity appealed to many Americans. More significantly, his campaign and presidency marked a turning point: for the first time, issues of substantial importance to Americans—and not mere party maneuvering—dominated national politics.

Though Cleveland brought about no significant policy changes, his emphasis on honesty and justice began to transform the spirit of American politics. His administration eventually proved to skeptical Republicans that a Democrat in the White House would not undo the accomplishments of the war, and the country's factional disputes finally began to cool.

New Frontiers

THE DEMOCRATS RENOMINATED CLEVELAND IN 1888.
When James Blaine declined the Republican nomination, party
leaders selected U.S. senator Benjamin Harrison, grandson of former
president William H. Harrison (who served for only one month
before his death in April 1841). A popular war hero and a fine public
speaker, Harrison advocated civil-service reform, federal regulation
of railroads and trusts, and a high tariff to protect American industry.

As expected, the tariff issue dominated the 1888 presidential
campaign. Republicans claimed that by calling for reduced tariffs,
Cleveland advocated "free trade" among all countries and favored
foreign interests over domestic. His opponents made personal attacks
as well, accusing him of drinking and wife beating.

In what may have been the most corrupt presidential campaign in
U.S. history, filled with bribes and slander on both sides, the final
blow to Cleveland's campaign was the "Murchison letter" scandal.
Falling into a carefully planned Republican trap, the British minister
to Washington, Sir Lionel Sackville-West, wrote a letter advising

The inauguration of President Benjamin Harrison—the "Centennial President"—on March 4, 1889. Though filled with corruption and mudslinging, the 1888 presidential campaign marked the first time in U.S. history that a candidate directly addressed voters on political issues.

George A. Osgoodsby, an office-seeking government employee and a naturalized American citizen of English birth, to vote for Cleveland. This evidence of foreign intervention in American affairs was viewed by critics as further proof of the president's overzealous support of free trade.

But the election was not all scandal. In a unique and unexpected "front-porch campaign," Harrison delivered more than 80 speeches to hundreds of thousands of people who visited him in his hometown of Indianapolis, Indiana. Despite the corruption and mudslinging, the contest of 1888 significantly changed the way American political campaigns were run: for the first time, a candidate directly addressed voters. Benjamin Harrison became the "Centennial President"—inaugurated in 1889, 100 years after George Washington was elected.

During the second half of the 19th century, America grew from the original 13 colonies into a vast nation, stretching from California to Maine—45 states in all. Nowhere was this expansion more rapid than in the land west of the Mississippi River.

The passage of the Homestead Act in 1862 allowed settlers to acquire thousands of acres of "public domain" land to establish new farms, and the country spread westward. The Industrial Revolution of the 1870s provided the tools to farm the vast midwest region known as the Great Plains: machinery for large-scale farm operations, roads for transportation, and windmills for water. By the close of the century, pioneers in search of gold and mining land had reached the West Coast, and the last frontier for American settlers—the Far West—vanished.

America was not finished growing, however. The country was already rich in natural resources and investment capital (an accumulation of wealth or goods that is invested to earn more income) and had a well-developed transportation system. With industrialization, the United States became a manufacturing power. The new industry also depended

heavily on immigrant laborers seeking improved working and living conditions. Between 1865 and 1917, more than 25 million immigrants arrived in the United States, mostly from European countries.

The Industrial Revolution transformed the national economy. The U.S. Census Report of 1900 declared that America's principal source of wealth up until about 1890 was agriculture. By 1919—only 30 years later—the country's annual manufacturing revenue was three times that of agriculture.

Increased productivity demanded a search for new markets for surplus products and new sources of raw materials and investment capital. Having reached the limits of its own land, the United States followed the lead of European nations with colonies in Africa and Asia and began the quest for new territory by looking outward, toward other lands and continents. This process of extending political or economic control over foreign territories became known as imperialism.

The search for new markets was only one reason for America's rapid accumulation of foreign territory. Another was the prevailing belief in a philosophy known as Manifest Destiny. The phrase was first used in an 1845 journal article by John L. O'Sullivan. Referring to America's recent annexation of Texas, O'Sullivan declared that it was the country's "manifest destiny to overspread the continent allotted by Providence for the free development of our yearly multiplying millions." The idea of a divinely sanctioned right to acquire land had popular appeal, and Manifest Destiny would be used by advocates of other annexations, including the Oregon Territory during a dispute with Great Britain and the Mexican Territory following the Mexican War (1846-48).

Manifest Destiny had an impact on many other fields of human studies as well. Historians like John Fiske and John W. Burgess discussed the concept as it related to racial issues, while Josiah Strong believed it applied also to faith and religion: the Anglo-Saxon, Strong declared, was

(continued on page 45)

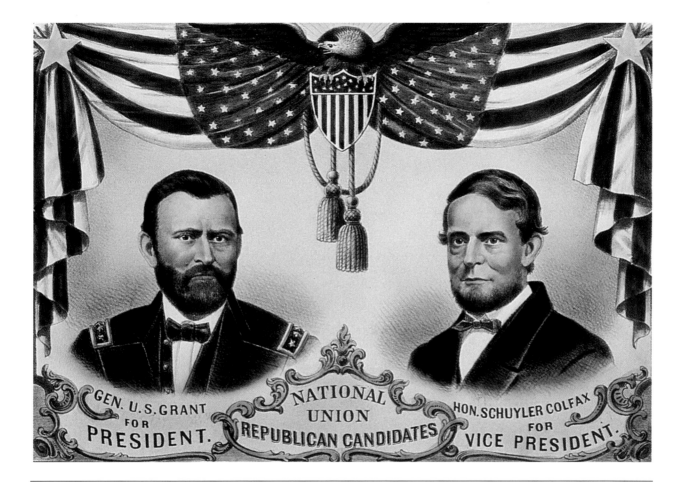

An 1868 election poster for the National Union Republican candidates Ulysses S. Grant and Schuyler Colfax. Republican party leaders adopted the name "National Union" after the reverses of the Civil War convinced them that it was necessary to broaden the party base. Grant won the election; after he was renominated in 1872, the more liberal elements of the party broke away and took the name Liberal Republican party, nominating Horace Greeley for president. Grant was reelected by a substantial margin.

A commemorative badge for James A. Garfield, who was president for only four months when he was assassinated on July 2, 1881.

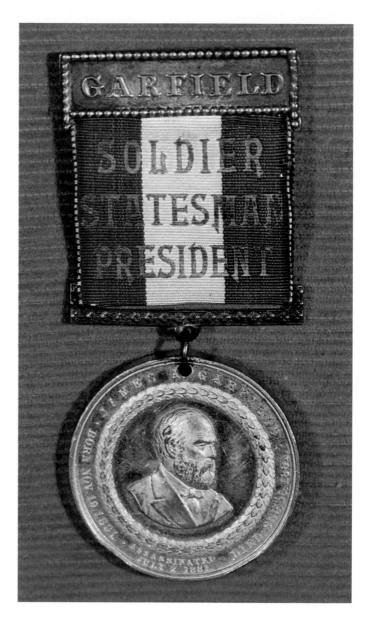

This colorful 1882 lithograph showing scores of political figures as elements in a Fourth of July fireworks display is typical of the skewering that many political officials received during the Gilded Age. Tammany Hall is depicted below the pyrotechnics, with Boss Tweed in a circle to the left. Also shown are references to the Star Route scandal, in which a ring of officials much like the Tweed Ring grossly inflated the service costs of paying postal carriers and divided the profits when contracts were paid.

James G. Blaine as a sailor clinging to the mast of a protectionist ship. This illustration refers to Blaine's advocacy of the Chinese Exclusion Act of 1882, which banned Chinese immigration for 10 years. Later laws excluded all Asian immigration, until in 1943 the acts were repealed and U.S. citizenship privileges were extended to Chinese.

(continued from page 40)

"divinely commissioned to be, in a peculiar sense, his brother's keeper."

Charles Darwin, the famous British naturalist, seemed to acknowledge the concept of Manifest Destiny in nature itself. Just as the fittest species would survive, he said, so the most deserving of nations would prevail:

> There is apparently much truth in the belief that the wonderful progress of the United States, as well as the character of the people, are the results of natural selection. . . . the more energetic, restless and courageous men from all parts of Europe having emigrated during the last ten or twelve generations to that great country and having there succeeded best.

Originally embraced by the Democratic party, the concept of Manifest Destiny was eventually adopted by Republicans. At the turn of the century, it was used to justify the annexations of Hawaii and Guam.

Not all Americans approved of foreign expansion, however. Among those most affected by the booming manufacturing business and the search for new markets were the nation's farmers. Newly invented machinery enabled them to increase productivity and cultivate larger areas of land than ever before. As a result, farmers began producing more than the country could consume, and the surplus was sold to foreign consumers. The American farmer became more dependent for his income on middlemen—those who handled and transported his products to distant markets.

The predicament of the American farmer was central to the 1892 presidential campaign. Overproduction created a surplus of goods but also drove prices down. Irregular currency regulations and tariffs created more difficulties. Moreover, because farmers were forced to rely nearly completely on railroads for transportation, they often faced excessive duty taxes and unprincipled middlemen as well.

Disappointed and angry with the government's failure to correct these problems, farmers began organizing themselves. The National Grange was founded in the 1870s as a social and community-service organization for farmers. By the 1880s, the Grangers had begun drafting their own objectives for legislation and in 1887, they were instrumental in the creation of Congress's Interstate Commerce Commission, which ensured "reasonable and just" railroad rates.

To strengthen self-reliance and to reduce the power of middlemen, the Grangers also established cooperatives—groups of farmers who jointly owned stores, grain elevators, insurance companies, and other enterprises and who combined their goods for sale. Members of cooperatives also appointed agents to deal directly with manufacturers and suppliers of farm equipment.

On May 19, 1891, the People's Party debuted at a convention in Cincinnati, Ohio. Known also as Populists, the members of the agricultural-based party derived their policies from the Grangers: increased railroad regulation, banking reforms, and government loans. They nominated James B. Weaver of Iowa, a Civil War veteran and former Republican congressman, as their presidential candidate.

Weaver received only one million popular votes and 22 electoral votes in the election, in which Democrat Grover Cleveland again became president. But the presence of a third party had substantially altered the face of national politics. For the first time, politicians realized that dissatisfied Democrat and Republican voters could be lured away by a third party. By securing votes in key states or with influential interest groups, a third party might tip the scales that traditionally weighed only Democrat and Republican support—and possibly affect the outcome of the election itself.

The 1892 presidential election also heralded an important innovation in the American voting process: the secret ballot. Up to this time, ballots were printed and distributed to voters by party leaders or candidates themselves. Because voters were subject to pressure and intimidation, this system often produced fraudulent and unreliable vote tallies.

In an effort to eliminate corruption, 33 states adopted the ballot system developed in Australia during the 1850s. In this system, all candidates' names appear on a single, official ballot, which is printed at public expense and distributed at polling places. In this way, each citizen is also able to vote in secret. A November 1891 column in the Cincinnati Commercial Gazette colorfully described the vast improvement over the old voting system:

> Our citizens can be congratulated on the general conduct of the [election], offering so happy a contrast to the methods of a few years ago, when howling mobs surrounded many of the voting places, fighting within themselves, pulling and pushing voters about, and shamefully maltreating some; when even police officers took a hand in unlawful and unruly proceedings, and clubbed and dragged unoffending citizens to the station houses in order to prevent them from voting.

Grover Cleveland had no sooner won the presidential election than disaster struck. Ten days before he assumed office, the huge Philadelphia and Reading Railroad Company abruptly declared bankruptcy, sending shock waves through the New York Stock Exchange. On May 5, 1893, another large firm, the National Cordage Company, went bankrupt,

An early meeting of the National Grange, 1873. Originally a social and community-service association for farmers, the Grangers became politically active in the 1880s. The People's Party, established in 1891, was founded on their policies.

The introduction of the Australian secret ballot system for the 1892 presidential election greatly reduced voter fraud and unreliable tallies. Here, a sample of an official ballot printed by the government is shown beneath an illustration of the new voting process.

and the national market collapsed. In the panic that followed, 500 banks and nearly 16,000 businesses went under before year's end; within a year after Cleveland's inauguration, 4 million (out of a population of 65 million) were unemployed.

During this period, the United States currency system operated on what is called the gold standard—that is, the value of U.S. currency was backed by a government supply of gold. And because the United States was now part of a larger market, financial decisions elsewhere in the world affected its economy. So when British investors sought gold in exchange for American investments, the demand depleted the U.S. gold reserve.

To keep the reserve from falling too low, Cleveland had the U.S. Treasury sell government bonds to a group of New York bankers in exchange for gold. Although the move was effective, many Americans were dismayed that the national government had grown dependent on a group of Wall Street bankers. As a result, Cleveland alienated many members of his own party and his popularity suffered greatly.

More troubles awaited Cleveland. In 1894, economic conditions led George Pullman, head of the Pullman Palace Car Company, a passenger train business, to lay off 3,000 of 5,800 employees. Pullman then reduced the wages of the remaining workers without lowering the rent on their housing, which he also owned. On June 26, Eugene V. Debs of the American Railway Union launched a boycott of all Pullman cars in sympathy for the protesting workers. Railroads retaliated by firing union members, and the union struck, disabling railroads across the country.

In this sketch, President Grover Cleveland is seen on the far right bowing to the concerns of extravagantly attired eastern businessmen, who claim poverty and deprivation after the panic of 1893. The parade is led by steel magnate Andrew Carnegie and millionaire merchant John Wanamaker, who march under a banner depicting not an American eagle but a vulture. The businessmen are shown disembarking from the "Pullman Train."

On July 3, the rebellion quickly attracted the attention of the public—and of the new president—when striking workers interrupted postal delivery by destroying a mail train. An enraged President Cleveland ordered federal troops into Chicago to break the strike. "If it takes every dollar in the Treasury and every soldier in the United States to deliver a postal card in Chicago," he thundered, "that postal card

should be delivered." By July 20, federal troops had been withdrawn, but the trains were operating under military guard. The union had been defeated by the government.

As the depression and the Pullman strike clearly demonstrated, the nation's economy was no longer simply a scattered group of small producers selling to local markets. It had become a vast, single market, tied together by railroads and dominated by a handful of large firms that sold to the world. Because of this immense shift in the nation's economic foundation, the presidential election of 1896 was critical in the national struggle between agrarian and industrial interests.

Battleships and Comic Strips

WITH THE NATION'S ECONOMIC SITUATION IN MIND, Republicans chose William McKinley, a former congressman and governor of Ohio, for their presidential candidate in 1896. McKinley believed that a gold standard for currency and protective tariffs would help restore American prosperity. He advocated tax reform, including higher rates for corporations, and regarded the formation of a national —not sectional—policy as critical to the nation's economic recovery.

Democrats, on the other hand, championed the eloquent William Jennings Bryan, who advocated a return to what was called bimetallism, a monetary standard based on both gold and silver that was used in the United States until 1873. American farmers, silver-mine owners, and debtors—mostly Democrats—believed that by allowing silver to be mined in unlimited quantities at no charge to the mine owner, the U.S. Treasury would be able to circulate a huge volume of new currency. This in turn would bring economic justice to agrarian interests, who could not compete in power and government influence with big businesses. But gold-standard advocates—mostly Republicans—

President William McKinley delivers his inaugural address on March 4, 1897. McKinley ran a successful "front-porch" campaign that enabled him to win the majority of popular votes—the first winning candidate to do so in 16 years.

argued that the return to bimetallism represented an unscrupulous agrarian plan to overcome debts.

Bimetallists, or "free-silver" advocates, were somewhat successful: the Sherman Silver Purchase Act of 1890 decreed that the U.S. Treasury purchase 4.5 million ounces of silver each month at market price. During the panic of 1893, however, Cleveland had the act repealed—and sold U.S. government bonds to New York City bankers in exchange for gold —in his effort to halt declining gold reserves.

Cleveland's actions split the Democratic party into two factions—the more conservative gold standardists and the free-silverists—and Bryan, not Cleveland, was ultimately nominated. In what became known as his "Cross of Gold" speech during the Chicago Democratic National Convention, Bryan declared, "You shall not press down upon the brow of labor this crown of thorns. You shall not crucify mankind upon a cross of gold!"

But the Democratic candidate did not win the presidency. After a "front-porch" campaign that brought thousands of voters to his Ohio home, McKinley became the first winning candidate since 1872 to earn a majority of all votes cast and secured 271 electoral votes to Bryan's 176.

During his term in office, McKinley would sign an 1897 act raising tariffs and the Gold Standard Act of 1900, which declared gold the only standard of currency. But though these issues dominated the presidential campaign, foreign policy became the focus of McKinley's presidency. The United States had become a political world power by the turn of the century and the nation was growing increasingly concerned about protecting its interests abroad.

Foreign powers such as Great Britain were already experimenting with new, ironclad battleships and rifled guns (in which spiral grooves cut, or rifled, into the bore make the fired projectile more powerful).

A photograph of the remains of the destroyed U.S.S. *Maine* in Havana's harbor. The deaths of 260 Americans in the explosion convinced President McKinley to declare war on Spain.

But the U.S. Navy had fallen into serious disrepair, with slow, obsolete wooden cruisers armed with smooth-bore guns—and few battleships. By the 1880s, the British wit Oscar Wilde would ridicule the condition of the U.S. Navy in his book *The Canterville Ghost*, referring to it as one of the "ruins and curiosities" of America.

Admiral Alfred Thayer Mahan, author of the widely read book *The Influence of Sea Power upon History* (1890). Mahan's work induced federal legislators to increase funds to improve America's navy; by 1897 the United States had become a military power.

In 1883, during Chester A. Arthur's term of office, Congress authorized the purchase of four new steel cruisers and voted to cease major repairs on older ships. The birth of a new navy was at hand.

Seven years later, U.S. naval captain Alfred Thayer Mahan argued in his work *The Influence of Sea Power upon History: 1660-1783* that a strong naval presence was the key to success in international politics. The United States, he contended, must build a mighty battle fleet of ships that would gain control of the seas and prevent enemies from encroaching. Widely read by political leaders, Mahan's work persuaded many U.S. legislators to continue allocating funds toward improving the navy, so that by 1897, America had become a considerable military power.

Meanwhile, the spirit of Manifest Destiny was intensifying. The United States had already negotiated in 1872 with Samoa, an island nation in the southwest Pacific, for a U.S. naval station in a town called Pago Pago, on the Samoan island of Tutuila. And by 1891, America was showing interest in another territory: Hawaii.

By the 1890s, American sugar and mining interests exerted a powerful hold on Hawaii's economy and government. As with Samoa, the United States negotiated a treaty with Hawaii in 1887, establishing a naval base at Pearl Harbor on the island of Oahu. In 1893, reformers—many of them American—overthrew the Hawaiian monarchy and deposed Queen Liliuokalani. The following year, they formed a provisional government, placing Hawaii under the protection of the United States and declaring the islands a republic. Under President McKinley, the islands were annexed and became a U.S. territory in 1900.

But the principles of Manifest Destiny were not held exclusively by the United States. Though they did not view it as divinely inspired, other world powers such as Spain, Russia, and Germany began asserting the same right to freely acquire territory to expand an empire.

60

(continued on page 65)

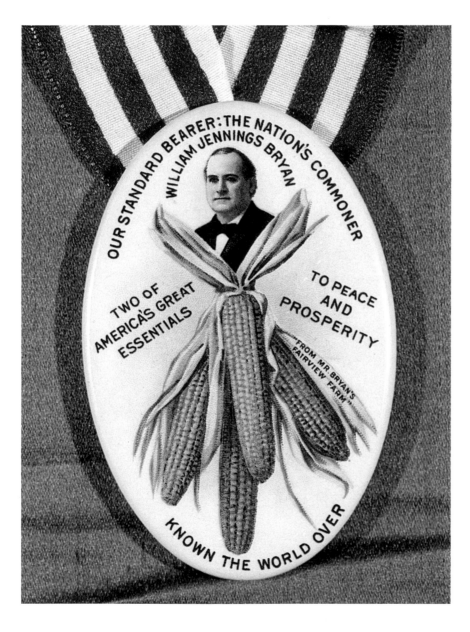

OUR STANDARD BEARER: THE NATION'S COMMONER
WILLIAM JENNINGS BRYAN

TWO OF AMERICA'S GREAT ESSENTIALS

TO PEACE AND PROSPERITY

"FROM MR. BRYAN'S FAIRVIEW FARM"

KNOWN THE WORLD OVER

This delegate's badge reflects William Jennings Bryan's status as the "Great Commoner" who consistently opposed special privileges for favored groups. Representing agrarian interests against big business and industrialism, Bryan ran for president three times on the Democratic ticket—first in 1896, when he delivered his famous "Cross of Gold" speech against the gold standard, again in 1900, and finally in 1908.

A gold standardist's view of the free-silver controversy: this 1886 illustration depicts Uncle Sam, or the United States, riding to national bankruptcy on a silver dollar bicycle.

The currency debate reached a climax during the 1896 presidential election, in which William McKinley won the Republican nomination over the opposition of conservative eastern "gold standardist" Republicans. Here he is shown being pulled by the "Eastern Gold Bug" businessman on the right and the "Western Silverite" farmer on the left. In 1900 President McKinley would sign the Gold Standard Act, which declared gold the only standard of currency.

A collection of 1904 campaign memorabilia for Republican Theodore Roosevelt showing the candidate as a "Rough Rider" in the Spanish-American War on one button and displaying the aims of his "Square Deal" on another. In the center is a metal pin shaped like Roosevelt's eyeglasses, called pince-nez.

(continued from page 60)

By 1894, Japan, like the United States, had become modernized; seeking to expand its Asian empire, Japan forced another Asian territory, Korea, into a treaty for independence. The agreement did not recognize China's informal sovereignty over Korea, however, and after much political maneuvering for control of the land, the two countries went to war. The Japanese crushed the Chinese forces in 1895, securing the Pescadores Islands, Taiwan, and Korea.

The Chinese-Japanese War did not go unnoticed. Many Western powers, including France, Germany, and the United States, were alarmed at Japan's swift victory and became anxious over the safety of their trading interests with China. In 1900, U.S. secretary of state John Hay dispatched messages to major powers—France, Germany, Great Britain, Italy, Japan, and Russia—asking each country to declare formally that it would not interfere in China's government and that it would abide by all existing rights to China's ports. Though all the nations evaded Hay's request (none would agree unless other nations complied), only Japan challenged it, and the Open Door agreement became international policy.

Another conflict was occurring closer to home. During the same period as the Chinese-Japanese War, Cuba, which had fought for independence from Spain during the Ten Years' War of 1868-78, was attracting attention in the United States with a renewed battle for freedom. Many Americans had heard reports of cruelty on the part of Spain toward the rebels and were sympathetic to the Cuban cause. But McKinley hesitated to involve U.S. troops.

At first the United States offered merely to mediate the conflict. But on February 15, 1898, the U.S.S. *Maine* was sunk near Havana by a mysterious explosion—attributed to a Spanish bomb—that killed 260 Americans. Shortly after, McKinley asked Congress to declare war on Spain.

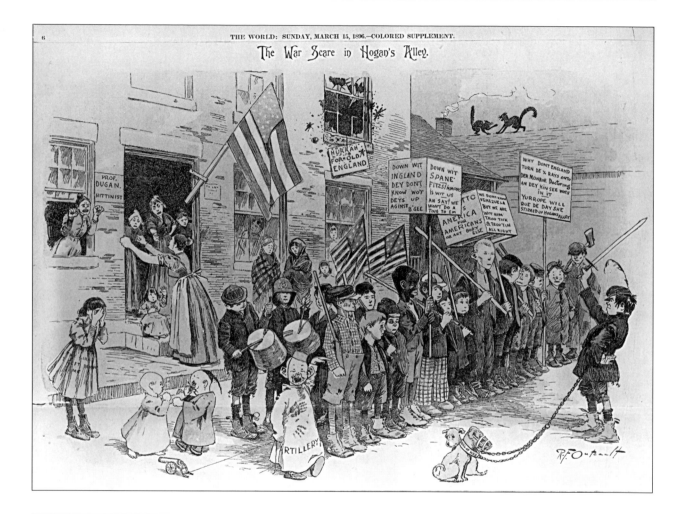

Richard Outcault's comic strip, "Hogan's Alley," which debuted in 1896 in the *New York World*. The "yellow kid" appears in the foreground.

This "splendid little war," as John Hay called it, lasted only 100 days, from April to August 1898—the shortest war in American history. The Spanish-American War would firmly establish the United States as a world power. No longer was intervention in foreign affairs condemned. America had invested $50 million in Cuban sugar and mining industries and by 1893, U.S. trade with Cuba was worth more than $100 million annually. Americans not only wanted Cuba to be free; they also wanted to protect their own foreign investments.

New York governor Theodore Roosevelt, one of the most outspoken proponents of imperialism, reflected this concern two years later, in 1900. "Greatness means strife for nation and man alike," he declared. "The guns of our war-ships in the tropic seas of the west and the remote east have awakened us to the knowledge of new duties. Our flag is a proud flag and it stands for liberty and civilization."

Most Americans learned of the strife in Cuba through the newspapers. Technological innovations in the printing process in the first half of the 19th century produced speedier presses and helped create a more literate American public. For the first time, books and periodicals would reach a mass market—a majority of readers.

The first modern-style newspaper in the United States, the *New York Herald*, was founded by James Gordon Bennett Sr. in 1835. Bennett organized a method of gathering news that is still used today: he sent reporters out on regular news "beats," established a corps of foreign correspondents, and created a band of reporters who exclusively covered national politics in Washington, D.C. He also pioneered the use of the telegraph to get the news out quickly.

Bennett was followed by other innovative newsmen, such as Horace Greeley, who in 1841 established the *New York Tribune*. In his newspaper, Greeley included an editorial page. Suddenly, it was possible for one

powerful voice to influence an entire country. By the turn of the century, the American press had become a powerful political instrument.

William Randolph Hearst, owner of the *New York Journal*, and Joseph Pulitzer, owner of the *New York World*, dominated American journalism beginning in the 1890s. The *World* developed the comic strip in 1889, and introduced color for the first time in 1893. Both papers thrived on flashy reporting, or sensationalism—a way of writing that deliberately seeks to arouse attention and interest with overemotional language. This flamboyance reached its peak during the Cuban rebellion against Spain.

As rivals in the same city, the *Journal* and the *World* competed for readers to increase circulation (the number of newspapers sold). Dispensing with balanced and unbiased reporting, the newspapers engaged in a notorious battle of their own: to increase readership, the papers deliberately set out to rouse sympathy for the Cuban rebels, creating false reports when no news was available. Often, headlines covered the entire half of a front page, with bright colors and misleading phrasing to attract attention. Filled with fiery proclamations—"Remember the *Maine*! To Hell with Spain!" became a rallying cry—the papers fanned the flames of anti-Spanish sentiment in the American public and helped drive the United States into war.

The two newspapers were also involved in a cartoon war that would ultimately give a name to such irresponsible journalism. In 1896, the *World* added yellow tint to the clothing of a cartoon character in the comic strip "Hogan's Alley." The character, a nameless young tenement dweller, became known as the "yellow kid." When Hearst observed how popular the character had become, he hired the cartoonist, Richard F. Outcault, to move the series to the *Journal*'s Sunday color section. Pulitzer countered by hiring another illustrator, George B. Luks, to continue the comic strip in the *World*.

But though circulation of both papers soared, the wildly sensational and often false reports about the Spanish-American War offended many readers—and other newspapers as well. Using the rival promotion of "yellow kids" as an image, Ervin Wardman, editor of the *New York Press*, wrote a column accusing both papers of yellow journalism— engaging in competition at the expense of fair reporting. The term is still used today.

Under terms of the Teller Amendment, passed by Congress when it declared war on Spain, the United States declared Cuba an independent country and pledged not to attempt to gain sovereignty over it. But the spirit of imperialism was strong in American government. By the terms of the 1899 Treaty of Paris, which officially ended the war, the United States temporarily occupied Cuba and acquired the Spanish territories of Puerto Rico, Guam, and the Philippines.

President McKinley had condemned Spain's seizure of Cuba as an act of "criminal aggression" in December of 1897. But the following year, despite strong criticism from many political groups, he maintained that it was necessary for America to secure the region to keep European interests out. "While we are conducting the war and until its conclusion we must keep all we get," he declared in May 1898. "When the war is over we must keep what we want."

The battle was not completely won, however. McKinley spent much of his remaining term suppressing a Filipino revolt in which thousands on both sides of the conflict ultimately perished. The loss of American life outraged many citizens and inflamed nationalist sentiments.

Meanwhile, more troubles arose in the Far East. Since their defeat by the Japanese and the establishment of the Open Door policy, many Chinese had become distrustful of foreigners—and of their

own government. An antigovernment society known as the Boxers (so named because they were originally a shadowboxing group) formed an alliance with government officials opposed to foreign influence. Tension between Boxers and the pro-foreign government intensified until, in early 1900, Boxer gangs began sweeping through northern Chinese towns, destroying Christian missions and attacking and killing Chinese Christians and foreign delegates. Foreign powers, anxious to protect their interests, sent battleships and troops to China, but by June the Boxer Rebellion had reached Peking (now known as Beijing) and the Chinese empress, sympathetic to the Boxer cause, declared war on the foreign powers.

By September 7, 1901, when the Chinese government and representatives of 11 world powers signed the Boxer Protocol, thousands of Chinese and foreigners had been killed and scores of Chinese towns pillaged. Among the terms of the agreement were the execution of 10 high officials in the Chinese government and a required "damage" payment to other countries of over $300 million.

Despite the turmoil of foreign affairs, McKinley's popular appeal remained strong and he was renominated for president in 1900. The only significant debate concerned the nomination of a running mate (Vice President Garrett A. Hobart had died the previous year). Members of the Republican convention chose New York governor Theodore Roosevelt for their vice-presidential candidate.

A charismatic and gregarious war hero, Roosevelt fascinated voters and became the sensation of the 1900 race. Youthful and energetic, he campaigned vigorously for the party. McKinley was reelected by a landslide, winning the greatest popular majority ever received up to that time by a presidential candidate.

Theodore Roosevelt, who became president following the assassination of William McKinley in 1901, delivers his 1905 inaugural address.

But Roosevelt's vigorous defense of U.S. imperialism alienated many, including party colleagues. Republican senator Mark Hanna of Ohio, McKinley's political advisor, had been among those who strongly opposed Roosevelt's nomination. Calling Roosevelt "that damned cowboy," he cried, "Don't any of you realize that there's only one life between this madman and the White House?"

Hanna's comment was chillingly prophetic: on September 6, 1901, an anarchist named Leon Czolgosz shot McKinley during a public reception in Buffalo, New York. McKinley died eight days later, and Roosevelt, at 42, became the youngest man ever to assume the office of president.

A Square Deal

SIX WEEKS SHY OF 43, "TEDDY" ROOSEVELT NONETHELESS brought a wealth of public-service experience to the Executive Office and a vibrant, determined spirit that many of his predecessors lacked. He had served as civil-service and police commissioner for New York City and was later elected governor of New York. As leader of the famed Rough Riders of the 1st U.S. Volunteer Cavalry in the Spanish-American War, he had become a larger-than-life character to many Americans.

In his inaugural speech, Roosevelt pledged to "continue, absolutely unbroken" McKinley's policies. But he also firmly reminded Americans that McKinley was no longer in office: "I am president," he declared. And one of his first actions was to transform the nature of the presidency itself.

The new president approached politics in the same way as he did the rest of his life, with energy and determination. He believed in living the "strenuous life," in which a person participates wholeheartedly, never shirking responsibility or retreating from

President Roosevelt is shown astride the Republican elephant in a railroad roundhouse, or repair station. Among many other reforms, Roosevelt's Hepburn Act of 1906 authorized the Interstate Commerce Commission to establish railroad rates and prohibit discrimination among shippers.

action. He personified a new kind of politician: glamorous, personable, and popular.

Roosevelt expanded the powers of the presidency by acting independently of Congress rather than working with it—and because Roosevelt was a widely popular leader, Congress was often compelled to support his reforms or risk popular disapproval. The United States Constitution, he declared, "must be interpreted, not as a straight jacket, not as laying the hand of death upon our development, but as an instrument designed for the life and healthy growth of the Nation."

President Roosevelt firmly believed that, as president, he represented all American citizens—farmers, businessmen, laborers, and office workers—and therefore had a moral responsibility to protect the interests of each one.

In an effort to maintain a balance among the concerns of these groups, he advocated tighter governmental control of big businesses. He called for regulations on trusts. He forced Congress to create the Bureau of Corporations to oversee U.S. corporations. In 1902, he persuaded the coal industry to settle a long-standing strike by agreeing to negotiate through an independent arbitrator—the first important pro-labor intervention by any U.S. president.

Under the Sherman Anti-Trust Act of 1890, which outlawed monopolies in interstate and foreign commerce, Roosevelt fearlessly initiated 25 antitrust proceedings, including one against the strongest trust in the country: the Northern Securities Company, a railroad group formed by powerful financiers like J. P. Morgan, John D. Rockefeller, and James J. Hill. He reinforced the Sherman Act by signing the Elkins anti-rebate railroad bill in 1903, which discontinued the railroads' practice of granting rebates on freight costs to favored customers.

Banker J. P. Morgan is caricatured here—with a train-shaped medallion dangling from his watch fob—as the owner of the "U.S. Sub-Treasury." Morgan founded a financial empire that profoundly influenced the American economy during the late 19th century. After the stock market crash of 1893, he became actively involved in financing railroads and reorganized several lines in the eastern United States. One of the business consolidations he created was the enormous Northern Securities Company, a railroad holding company that President Theodore Roosevelt dissolved under the 1890 Sherman Anti-Trust Act in 1904.

From the cab of a steam shovel, Roosevelt surveys the construction of the Panama Canal in 1906.

"Speak softly, and carry a big stick," Roosevelt often said, and he applied his own advice especially in foreign affairs. His earlier view— that America must fulfill its Manifest Destiny by establishing a worldwide empire—had softened. America was still a superior nation, Roosevelt maintained, but other nations could be equally powerful. At the same time, he was prepared at all times to protect U.S. foreign interests by force, and he built the U.S. Navy into a world power.

Roosevelt's most controversial action involved the country of Panama, an elongated strip of land, or isthmus, connecting Central and South America. The idea of building an artificial waterway across Panama to link the Atlantic and Pacific Oceans was centuries old. Traveling through the narrow isthmus—instead of around the entire South American continent—would shorten such a trip by about 7,000 miles and would eliminate several weeks of sea time.

But the technology to accomplish such an enormous undertaking was not available until the end of the 19th century. In 1878, the government of Colombia granted a French company the right to build a canal through Panama (at the time a Colombian province). Though work began in 1881, the hard rock of Panama was more difficult to cut through than had been thought, and epidemic malaria and yellow fever severely reduced the European labor force. In 1887, the French company went bankrupt and work on the canal ceased.

Seven years later, in an effort to salvage plans for the canal, another French company, Compagnie Nouvelle du Canal de Panama, resumed excavations in the isthmus. They had no sooner begun, however, than the U.S. Senate declared that their actions violated a U.S. policy known as the Monroe Doctrine.

Established in 1823 by President James Monroe, the Monroe Doctrine opposed European control or influence in the Western Hemisphere.

S. S. McClure, founder of *McClure's Magazine*, stands and chats with three of his contributors: from left, Willa Cather, Ida M. Tarbell, and Will Irwin. Tarbell was one of the first journalists to write articles exposing unethical corporate and political practices. This new style of reporting launched a wave of investigative journalism, or "muckraking," aimed at uncovering and eliminating corruption in government and business.

Where American "rights and interests" were involved, Monroe declared, the United States would consider any attempt by European countries to "extend their system to any portion of this hemisphere as dangerous to our peace and safety." Such acts, he declared, would be viewed as "the manifestation of an unfriendly disposition toward the United States."

By 1902, Compagnie Nouvelle du Canal de Panama, eager to recover its losses after being forced to halt work on the canal, agreed to sell its holdings to the United States, provided the United States secured an agreement from Colombia. Secretary of State John Hay then approached Colombian ambassador Tomás Herrán, offering $10 million and a $250,000 annual rental fee for the creation of the Panama Canal Zone, a 10-mile-wide strip of land that the United States would control completely "in perpetuity" (forever). Colombia refused to ratify the agreement.

In November of 1903, Panamanian revolutionaries, who had long sought independence and were angered by the Colombian government's rejection of the U.S. treaty, organized a revolt. The uprising, which was quietly encouraged by France and the United States, was ultimately successful. By month's end, Panama was formally recognized as an independent country. The treaty granting America rights to the Panama Canal Zone — known as the Hay-Bunau-Varilla Treaty (Philippe Bunau-Varilla owned the French canal company) — was ratified in 1904.

The Panama Canal opened 10 years later, on August 15, 1914. By invoking the Monroe Doctrine and tacitly endorsing a Panamanian revolution, Roosevelt had alienated not only Colombia but many Latin American countries as well. His forceful use of U.S. power to gain control over foreign interests became known as "bully diplomacy."

Though the United States controlled the Panama Canal Zone, it did

not own the land. Despite his actions in Panama, Roosevelt had little desire to establish control over the Caribbean; in 1902, for example, he had withdrawn American troops from Cuba. But Roosevelt also refused to allow interference from European powers. In 1903 he warned Germany to stay out of Venezuela, a South American country. The following year, fearing European interference in Latin America, the president formulated what is known as the "Roosevelt Corollary" to the Monroe Doctrine. Only the United States, he declared, had the right to take action in Latin American countries, and then only in extreme circumstances:

> Chronic wrongdoing . . . may in America, as elsewhere, ultimately require intervention by some civilized nation, and in the Western Hemisphere the adherence of the United States to the Monroe Doctrine may force the United States, however reluctantly, in flagrant cases of such wrongdoing or impotence, to the exercises of an international police power.

Using this reasoning, the United States took control of the bankrupt and corrupt Dominican Republic in 1904. Roosevelt expressed his reluctance, declaring that he felt as much inclination to annex the Dominican Republic as "a gorged boa constrictor might have to swallow a porcupine wrong-end-to."

Roosevelt soundly defeated his Democratic opponent, Alton B. Parker, in the 1904 presidential election, winning the greatest number of popular votes up to that time and sweeping the electoral college, 336 to 140. Even big businessmen like J. P. Morgan and John D. Rockefeller,

whose trust Roosevelt had crushed, supported him, asserting that the "impulsive candidate of the party of conservatism" (Roosevelt) was preferable to the "conservative candidate of the party which the business interests regard as permanently and dangerously impulsive" (Parker).

Many congressmen—including older members of Roosevelt's own party—continued to see the president as a renegade and tried to block many of his reform proposals. Nevertheless, during his second administration, he relied on the power of popular approval to enact an impressive body of legislation, which he called his "Square Deal."

Roosevelt continued to maintain that every American was entitled to fair treatment by the federal government. One of his first successes was the Hepburn Act of 1906, authorizing the Interstate Commerce Commission (ICC) to establish railroad rates and prohibit discrimination among shippers.

That same year, he secured similar regulations for industry, winning approval for the Pure Food and Drug Act and the Meat Inspection Act. The appalling working conditions and filthy handling practices of the meat industry were made public in 1906 by writer Upton Sinclair in his novel *The Jungle*, a tale of an immigrant worker in the Chicago stockyards:

> [A] man could run his hand over these piles of meat and sweep off handfuls of the dried dung of rats. These rats were nuisances, and the packers would put poisoned bread out for them, they would die, and then rats, bread, and meat would go into the hoppers together.

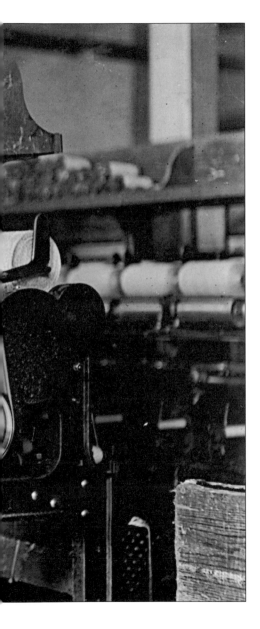

Young boys tending to machinery in a textile mill. At the turn of the century, the minimum age for child workers was 12 and the maximum workday was 10 hours; however, employers routinely ignored the laws. During Roosevelt's administration, the National Child Labor Committee was formed to help eliminate such abuses.

The Meat Inspection Act required federal inspection of meats and imposed strict sanitation measures upon all meat industries.

The president took steps to reform labor practices as well. At the turn of the century, it was common practice to employ very young children as laborers. With no legal recourse and no power, children worked under dangerous conditions and for long hours. The National Child Labor Committee, established in 1904, fought to prevent forced employment of underage workers. And by 1914, most states had enacted laws establishing a legal minimum age for workers and limiting the number of hours they were permitted to work.

One of Roosevelt's most important causes was the conservation of America's national resources. With intense dedication, the president overcame both popular and political opposition to enact sweeping laws protecting the nation's forests, waters, mineral deposits, and wildlife.

In 1902, Roosevelt supported the Democratic-sponsored Newlands Act, which initiated 30 irrigation projects across the country. In 1905, he reorganized the federal Forest Service, enacted federal safety measures for privately owned waterpower companies, and put into reserve 125 million acres of national forest—three times what had been put aside by Presidents Harrison, Cleveland, and McKinley combined. He convinced many lumber companies to change their cutting methods to prevent deforestation, and placed coal and mineral deposits under federal regulation.

Roosevelt did not stop there. He doubled the number of national parks to 10, created 16 national monuments, and established 51 wildlife refuges. So vast were his achievements that a longtime adversary, Republican senator Robert M. LaFollette, declared Roosevelt the pioneer of "a world movement for . . . saving for the human race the things on which alone a peaceful, progressive, and happy life can be founded."

The president was not alone in his zeal to improve American institutions. A popular movement known as Progressivism had arisen around 1900. Like the earlier Populist party, the Progressives condemned big business's overly strong influence on government policy and its effect on the political and economic freedom of American laborers. Like Roosevelt, the Progressives advocated strict regulation of big business as the first major step toward widespread reform.

Many Americans first learned of political and economic corruption through newspapers and magazines. In 1902, *McClure's Magazine*, founded in 1893 by Irish immigrant S. S. McClure, began publishing a series of articles by Ida M. Tarbell exposing unscrupulous practices in the Standard Oil Company. The following year, *McClure's* published more articles on municipal (local government) and labor corruption. And in 1904, Lincoln Steffens, another *McClure's* writer, reported on city and state politics in the same way. Traveling across the country to cities like St. Louis, Chicago, Pittsburgh, Philadelphia, and New York, Steffens discovered an alarmingly strong link between big business and local politics. In a series of articles called "The Shame of the Cities," Steffens wrote:

> When I set out to describe the corrupt systems of certain typical cities, I meant to show simply how the people were deceived and betrayed. But . . . the startling truth lay bare that corruption was not merely political, it was financial, commercial, social, the ramifications of boodle [money] were so complex, various and far-reaching that one mind could hardly grasp them. . . . Can a city be governed without any alliance with crime? It was an open question.

Reports like Tarbell's and Steffens's sparked a crusade of what we might today call investigative journalism—writing that aims to expose, and thereby help to eliminate, political corruption. Between 1902 and 1912, over 1,000 such articles appeared in the nation's magazines.

Though a reformist himself, Teddy Roosevelt did not entirely approve of such reporting. Using a phrase from John Bunyan's 17th-century allegory, *Pilgrim's Progress*, Roosevelt began calling it "muckraking." (In the story, one character spends his time using a "muck-rake" to rake dirt and garbage on the ground, rather than looking upward toward nobler things.) Roosevelt feared that constant emphasis on political corruption was not the way to correct it and could stir dangerous public unrest. "There is filth on the floor," he admitted in a 1906 speech, "and it must be scraped up with the muck-rake." But, he continued,

> [T]he man who never does anything else, who never thinks or speaks or writes, save of his feats with the muck-rake, speedily becomes, not a help to society, not an incitement to good, but one of the most potent forces of evil.

Despite Roosevelt's reservations, the muckrakers helped increase public support for many of his policies, like the Pure Food and Drug Act, the Meat Inspection Act, and the Hepburn Act. Many reporters were proud of the name, and all believed they provided an important service to the American public.

They were correct. Through muckraking journalism and the strength and determination of President Roosevelt, Americans grew increasingly aware of the country's need for reform and of the power of the government to bring about social, economic, and political improvement. The U.S. government had come a long way from the abuses of the Reconstruction era, and a much longer road lay ahead. But Theodore Roosevelt's vision of an orderly, just, and efficient America was a remarkable beginning.

FURTHER READING

Cashman, Sean Dennis. *America in the Gilded Age: From the Death of Lincoln to the Rise of Theodore Roosevelt*. New York: New York University Press, 1988.

Cooper, John Milton, Jr. *Pivotal Decades: The United States, 1900-1920*. New York: W. W. Norton & Company, 1990.

————. *The Warrior and the Priest: Woodrow Wilson and Teddy Roosevelt*. Cambridge, MA: Belknap Press of Harvard University Press, 1983.

Faulkner, Harold U. *Politics, Reform, and Expansion: 1890-1900*. New York: Harper & Row, 1959.

Garraty, John A. *The New Commonwealth: 1877-1890*. New York: Harper & Row, 1968.

Goldman, Eric. *Rendezvous with Destiny: A History of Modern American Reform*. New York: Knopf, 1966.

Gould, Lewis L. *The Presidency of Theodore Roosevelt*. Kansas City: University Press of Kansas, 1991.

Hofstadter, Richard, ed. *The Progressive Movement: 1900-1915*. New York: Simon & Schuster, Inc., 1966.

Hoover, Herbert. *The Ordeal of Woodrow Wilson*. New York: McGraw-Hill, 1958.

Keller, Morton. *Affairs of State: Public Life in Late 19th-Century America*. London: Belknap, 1977.

Lord, Walter. *The Good Years: From 1900 to the First World War*. New York: Harper & Row, 1960.

Socolofsky, Homer E., and Allan B. Spetter. *The Presidency of Benjamin Harrison*. Kansas: University Press of Kansas, 1987.

Tindall, George Brown. *America: A Narrative History*. New York: W. W. Norton & Company, Inc., 1984.

Wiebe, Robert H. *The Search for Order, 1877-1920*. New York: Hill and Wang, 1967.

INDEX

PICTURE CREDITS

page

10:	Library Of Congress, #62-33270
12:	Library Of Congress, #62-53830
13:	Library Of Congress
14:	The Bettmann Archive
16-17: Library Of Congress, #62-57524
21:	The BettmannArchive
26:	Schomburg Center For Research In Black Culture, NYPL
27:	Corbis-Bettmann
28:	Corbis-Bettmann
29:	Library Of Congress, #62-34243
31:	Corbis-Bettmann
34:	The Bettmann Archive

38:	Corbis-Bettmann

Color Section
41:	The Bettmann Archive
42:	The Bettmann Archive
43:	The Bettmann Archive
44:	The Bettmann Archive

48-49: Library Of Congress, #62-3430
50:	The Bettmann Archive
52:	The Bettmann Archive
53:	Library Of Congress, #62-3526
56:	Library Of Congress, #62-237
58:	Library Of Congress, #62-11020
59:	The Bettmann Archive

Color Section
61:	The Bettmann Archive
62:	The Bettmann Archive
63:	The Bettmann Archive
64:	The Bettmann Archive
66:	Library Of Congress, #62-34208
71:	Corbis-Bettmann
74-75: Library Of Congress, #62-10353
77:	The Bettmann Archive
78:	Corbis-Bettmann
80:	UPI/Corbis-Bettmann
84-85: Library Of Congress, #62-23944

JOHN C. HAVENS is an actor and writer living in New York City. He is making his Broadway debut in the new musical *Steel Pier*. He is currently working on other nonfiction titles and a novel.

Contains a clear, vivid and brilliant narrative of the events of our history, from the discovery of the American continent down to the present time. It gives a most interesting account of the **Indians of North America** from the time of the coming of the white men. Every step of our **colonial history** is traced with patient fidelity, and the sources of those noble and, we trust, enduring institutions, which have made our country h with remarkable clear-ear and succinct account or independence, and the eral Union, the events of e of the revolution to the on. 960 pages, 500 fine encloth, marbled edges.
............**$3.50**
............**$1.50**
8c. extra.

ROBERTS RULES OF ORDER

es of ve as-rules , conth all cieties sities. and ins a hair-stions turn-

$0.75
0.52
ents, extra.

h **Self-Taught.** A new le principles, for universal h pronunciation of every the acquirement of the dered less laborious and y any of the old methods.
............**20c**
ge, 2c.

n **Self-Taught.** Uniform ht," and arranged in ac-principle of thoroughness
............**20c**

h **Self-Taught.** A book of panish language, arranged ethod as the "French" and author and uniform with himm..............**$0.20**
2 cents.

Self-Taught. Uniform in hree foregoing books. By
............**$0.20**
3 cents.

e Sense of 3,000 French his ingenious little book ll that its title claims. It at least three thousand guage, forming a large pro-n ordinary conversation, y the same as in English, y very slight and easily their termination. 16mo. s..............**$0.20**
3 cents.

n **Self-Taught.** A new e principles, for universal e pronunciation of every the acquirement of the dered less laborious and

No. 6626. Prescription Scales. A polished cherry or walnut box, with drawer; has pillar and 6-in. beam, 2⅛-inch pans and full set of weights; weight, 1¼ lbs. Price.....**$2.25**

No. 6626.

No. 6627. Prescription Scales with pillar and 8 inch beam, on polished walnut box with drawer, nickel plated, pans 2¾ in. diameter, brass work lacquered; has full set of weights. Price..............**$3.75**
Scale No. 6627 can be taken apart and packed in drawer of the stand.

FLASH LAMP.

No. 6630. The "James" Flash Lamp is the simplest yet most practical device ever invented for burning flash light powders of all kinds. It dispenses entirely with the use of alcohols gasoline, etc. The powder is ignited with a common parlor match by simply pulling the trigger with the finger when you are ready. The action lights the match which is forced by a spring into the powder in the flash pan exploding it. The charge of powder can be governed to suit the requirements.
Price..............**$1.60**

Harvard Book Holders.

An ornament to the home, office and library. No wood-work used in their construction. A holder we highly recommend. The sides are operated by double acting springs, the book being firmly clamped while closed, and resting upon a level surface when open. The adjustment to books of differ-sizes and the inclination to any angle or slant are effected by a single screw. They are adjustable to different heights, and are easily set up. They are warranted not to break or get out of order with ordinary use, and after years of proper use will be as good as new.
52000 Complete with casters and revolving book shelf. Nickel Plated and highly polished or antique copper. Price..............**$3.85**
52002 Complete with casters and Revolving Book Shelf and finished in rubber, Japan or bronze. Price..............**$2.10**
52003 One same style as No. 52000 but no shelf or casters. Price..............**$1.85**

Dictionary and Book Holders.

Cannot be broken with ordinary usage. The edges of the covers are protected by felt-lined guards, and the rests are so made that the book cannot get out of

(right column)

single screw. They are adjustable to different heights, and are easily set up. They are warranted not to break or get out of order with ordinary use, and after years of proper use will be as good as new.
52000 Complete with casters and revolving book shelf. Nickel Plated and highly polished or antique copper. Price..............**$3.85**
52002 Complete with casters and Revolving Book Shelf and finished in rubber, Japan or bronze. Price..............**$2.10**
52003 One same style as No. 52000 but no shelf or casters. Price..............**$1.85**

Noyes' Dictionary and Book Holders.

Cannot be broken with ordinary usage. The edges of the covers are protected by felt-lined guards, and the rests are so made that the book cannot get out of shape.
52008. Noyes' adjustable Book Holder with book rack, bronze. Price..............**$2.10**
52010 With Book Rack to hold two volumes, bronze. Price..............**$3.25**

No. 52010. No. 52008.

Globes.

For offices, homes, libraries, or the school room these globes **are the best in the country** at the price we offer them.

It would be impossible to place too much emphasis upon the fact that the covers used upon these globes, all sizes, **are from new plates.** Every improvement in engraving, printing, coloring and mounting the maps has received **critical attention,** and the latest geographical changes are correctly shown.

A copy of the **Globe Manual** will occompany each globe.

The Manual Gives Explanations of the Terms Used in Geography and Astronomy, and the phenomena of mathematical geography, including **temperature and ocean currents,** and forty-six problems on the use of globes, with rules and illustrative examples; also several valuable tables.

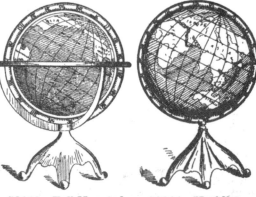

52012. Full Mounted.   **52014. Meridian.**